Stepping Into Faith

Prayer Journaling Through The Eyes of a Dancer

By Debbie Welch

Find More Inspiration at:
SteppingIntoFaith.com
Questions? Comments?
Contact Debbie Welch at:
dwelch@steppingintofaith
We hope you enjoy this journal and will leave
a 5 star review and some kind words.

Stepping Into Faith
Prayer Journaling Through
The Eyes Of A Dancer

Copyright © 2019 by Debbie Welch
& New Fair Haven Publishing
Chicago, IL & Dallas, TX

Scriptures are taken for the King James Version of the Bible

Book and Cover Design by New Fair Haven Publishing
a Chayil Enterprises, LLC Company, Dallas, Texas

For more books like this visit
https://NewFairHavenPublishing.com
Editor: Rhonda DeYampert

ISBN: 978-0-578-52119-0

A SPECIAL DEDICATION

To My Children, Grandchildren & Their Children

My Angels I love you more than you will ever know. You are the foundation of my being. God chose you carefully when He delivered you to me. You are all a reflection of my strength because you stand tall and walk with confidence in your beliefs. You have compassion for others around you and you live life through passion and celebration. I thank God for your gifts of laughter that we share often. I am forever grateful to God for your creation and for you all, your gift to me.

From the first time I saw each of your bright shining eyes, I fell in love with you! I knew that God had poured favor upon me because your blessings were all so special. You have all wrecked my heart with a love that cannot be explained, you are truly my reason for being.

Please understand that each day may not be the same, you will have some great days when everything seems clear and some that are not so clear, they may seem foggy and unbearable. Know that God can make the journey a lot clearer if you just believe. Don't be afraid to pray and ask Him to help you when you are faced with unforeseen circumstances.

Start each day by giving thanks to Him for life, love and all the blessings that He has given you. Ask Him to protect your children as well as other children from evil and to keep them safe from harm. Pray a prayer to Him for the sick, the homeless, and those who are lost and far from Him. You will grow in your faith as you watch your prayers manifest not only for yourself but for others as well.

Each day God reminds me of the reasons to celebrate you with love. He trusts that I can be a good example of His light as it shines through me. I love spending time deep in prayer to God for your souls and praying for guidance, protection, strength and continued faith that you will one day come to know Him as I have. I'm forever grateful and thankful to Him who has given me this angel assignment. These writings and prayers are prayed in honor of you as you walk through your testimonies daily.

Forever in love with you,

Mom, Grandma and Great Grandma All In One

CONTENTS

Introduction:

What Is Stepping?

Courage

Trust

Faith

Healing

Strength

Joy

Patience

Friendship

Discernment

Love

Passion

Celebrate & Dance

About The Author

INTRODUCTION

What Is Stepping?

Not to be confused with today's Hip Hop Step, this dance, Stepping, is usually performed by a couple, moving to a step of six to eight counts. It is an urban dance that has spread past the city of Chicago into many metropolitan areas throughout the United States such as Atlanta, Miami, Milwaukee, New York, and Los Angeles to name a few.

The origins of Stepping can be traced to the 1930's dance known as the Jitterbug. A derivative of this form of dance evolved into the Chicago "bop" in the 1970's. Sam Chatman is credited as the person for giving this beloved dance style it's now familiar name and current moves - "The Chicago Step".

Gaining national attention, this dance ignited the dance world as it illuminates beauty, poise and grace as the gentleman leads the lady in a series of rhythmic steps. The dancers, called Steppers, are known for their stylish fashions. Couples put a lot of thought and care into what they wear to showcase the dance. Stepping highlights the female dance partner by making her the center attraction in the most respectful way.

Dancers travel throughout the United States to competitions that build community through networking opportunities. The love of the dance draws many to Stepping events so it's not necessary to have your own dance partner. Anyone can expect to find a connection on the dance floor!

Where most dances listen for the beat of the music, Steppers tune into the rhythm of the music which seems to be hidden somewhere just behind the beats and feels impossible to find for beginners.

Learning to Step is a challenge for novices, but with great instructional teaching, students find the joy of the dance as they put their steps in order on the dance floor.

Just like life, when we get anxious in our everyday walk in this world and everything seems so far away no matter how fast we move, sometimes it seems as if we just can't make "it" happen. The truth is, God does everything in steps, in order, without missing a beat. He counsels us that our steps through this life should be in order ("The steps of a good man are ordered by the Lord"-Psalm 37:23).

I hope that Stepping Into Faith, will bring you into your rhythm of life. As you read each section and begin to journal your thoughts and activities, may you find peace in your everyday walk with God.

The next time you feel overwhelmed, isolated, lonely, sad, afraid or anxious, revisit Stepping Into Faith as evidence of your victories contained in this prayer journal as you move through this world step by step!

*123*456*78*

Step, by Step, by Step

"I Hope You Dance".

COURAGE

Each day is an unfolding mystery. As we wander this life, it's easy to become paralyzed with uncertainty and feelings of being trapped in our own flesh. We forget how to appreciate and capture the 3D moments that are right in front of us because our attention gets captured by negativity and fear. This is the perfect time to ask God to enter our lives and help us push past those things that keep us from living life to the fullest.

It takes courage to move forward, when we need to make things happen; without it we will remain stunted in our growth, always waiting for someone else to rescue us and help us to get to the other side. We need to develop the courage to believe in God first knowing that He is the Almighty One and with Him on your side no one can break you, tear you down or block your blessings. Be fearless in your destiny and watch for the roadblocks as they are sure to be there. When necessary change your steps to keep the enemy of courage, fear and negativity, at bay.

Next Steps:

Many times, I've found myself up against a wall of uncertainty where fear tries to take ahold of my hopes and dreams. It is then I remember those beautiful words bestowed upon me through Christ, "Do not be afraid for I'm with you". The first step of bravery allows me to push past roadblocks with the endurance and stamina fueled by faith.

123*456*78 - Step With Courage

What are your greatest fears that keep you stuck? Identify any negative people, places and things that hold you back. How will you stand strong, tall and focused to receive all that God has for you? Write down your answers.

_____

_____

_____

_____

_____

Prayer:

"God please form a halo around me and protect me when I stand"

Scripture:

Be not afraid of sudden fear, neither of the desolation of the wicked, when it cometh. For the Lord shall be thy confidence, and shall keep thy foot from being taken. Withhold not good from them to whom it is due, when it is in the power of thine hand to do it. (Proverbs 3:25-27)

TRUST

Who can you really trust in a world filled with greed and lust? What a wonderful world it would be if we could believe everyone with open hands and hearts extended to the receiver without hesitation or disbelief. Although we may not be able to trust those in our day to day lives, we do have someone we can give our complete trust to and He is God.

I am reminded of a powerful scripture "God is not a man that He should lie" (Numbers 23:19). We can trust Him completely with our hearts knowing that He will always be gentle. Confess your weaknesses, tell Him your struggles, speak to Him boldly of your needs. He will listen without judgment and disappointment as you believe in His mercy. You can trust Him to know how to love you as He extends you grace through all of your trials.

Next Steps:

From a heart broken way too many times, trust has been a real struggle for me. I find myself questioning what is real and what is not more often than I should. It hurts deeply when you pour out your heart to find out those who you feel are in your corner are only there to see you fail; but I know that God wants me to forgive them and love them anyway. As I've grown in my faith, now I understand that I must guard my heart not from the world, but from the enemy that would try to steal my joy. So, I forgive, step back, and keep focused on dancing through life.

123*456*78 - Step With Confidence

Are there areas in your life that you have shut out the newness of life in order to guard your heart? What are they? How will you follow God's roadmap of trust by believing that He will guide you and reveal to you what is best for you?

_____

_____

_____

_____

_____

_____

_____

_____

Prayer:

"God please help me to discern good from evil."

Scripture:

Trust in the Lord with all thine heart; and do not lean unto thine own understanding. In all thy ways acknowledge him and he shall direct thy paths. (Proverbs 3:5-6)

.

FAITH

Releasing our hearts and souls to the will of God can sometimes be a struggle. The fear deeply embedded within our minds causes our hearts to pulsate like the locomotive of a fifteen-minute train when we are faced with scary or uncertain situations. Although we may have been taught to have faith in God, we can find ourselves in a place where we have not totally surrendered to God where He can fight our battles.

One must ask why it is so hard to give into God's total plan for our lives? Why are we so stuck in this area of growth? Is it that we are conditioned to only believe what we can see or is it that we feel inadequate as a child of God?

Next Steps:

Never could I imagined how my life would change the moment I stepped into faith twenty years ago during a Wednesday night church service. I was raised by my Grandmother in a Christian home where God's presence was always recognized. I was baptized at a young age and active in my church as a child, and I even sang in the choir.

As a child, living a Christian life was baby steps compared to now where I must exercise my faith – daily! Faith has matured me and now I understand the calling on my life and by stepping into faith I enjoy the reward of His unconditional love.

123*456*78 - Step With Trust

What are you believing God for? What is your part to make what you are hoping for happen?

_____

_____

_____

_____

_____

Prayer:

"God please give me a sign to know I'm not alone"

Scripture:

My brethren, count it all joy when yet fall into divers temptations; knowing *this*, that the trying of your faith worketh patience. But let patience have *her* perfect work, that Ye may be perfect and entire, wanting nothing. (James 1:2-4)

HEALING

Sickness, heartbreak or the loss of a love one can cause our hearts to become heavy and life seem suddenly unbearable. It is at these times that we must turn to God for strength and guidance. Know that He can bring us through the storms of life if we just believe in His love for us. God is the healer of all things. He removes the physical pain that comes with sickness, He mends broken marriages, and He watches over our children. God, and only God can turn any situation around for the good. Healing is a step-by step process so during these times, ask him to wrap you in his arms and allow His strength to envelope you. His grace will wash over your soul like a fierce ocean wave covering you with His blood to help weather the storm.

Next Steps:

Never underestimate Gods power to deliver healing when you've received a bad report. Last year I was preparing for a biopsy after my yearly mammogram showed a mass that needed to be removed (to determine if it was the big "C"). The morning of the biopsy, I entered in an unexplainable peace as I put my faith to work in Gods healing power. Long story short, in preparation for the biopsy I was having another ultrasound when the technician said, "I can't find it". The doctor entered the room and he too verified there was no mass. He couldn't explain it, he even stated "I have never seen anything like this". I wept with happiness saying, "only God ". Some in the room understood and came to embrace me. I was then sent for one last mammogram – again negative results. I am convinced that God stepped up to demonstrate who the real healer is.

123*456*78 - Step With Faith

Although your body may be weak to the culprit of sickness, just remember Jesus is the cure for all things and by His stripes we are healed. He has no degrees in medicine just an anointing from the Father to carry out His will to end your suffering. Do you totally believe in God's healing power in your life to deliver you and restore you? What areas in your life do you need healed? What steps will you take to demonstrate your faith in Gods healing power?

_____

_____

_____

_____

_____

_____

_____

_____

Prayer:

"God please cleanse my mind, body, soul and spirit of disease to give me new life"

Scripture:

Behold, I will bring it health and cure, and I will cure them, and we'll reveal unto them the abundance of peace and truth. (Jeremiah 33:6)

.

STRENGTH

Awaken each day and step out of bed with a pledge to overcome your obstacles no matter how big or small. Declare God as your frontline protection for you and your love ones. Do not give in to evil that lurks waiting for an opportunity to strike. Strengthen your faith to be an overcomer! Shape your tongue to speak victoriously and watch your energy level rise. Each day is a step in the right direction of building a strong foundation in the Lord!

Next Steps:

After losing my parents and grandparents at an early age, I became so afraid to face the world and how to figure everything out on my own. It was devastating believing that no one else would ever understand or love me the way they did. Life became a series of disappointments and pain and I became weaker in self-confidence and lost sight of who I was in Gods image. I began to cry out to Jesus to give me the strength I needed to face the dips and sways of life. God reminded me of His presence and that my loved ones were watching over me. With each passing day I step into a new kind of strength - one that continues to remind me that my Jesus will always provide me the strength I need for any situation.

123*456*78 - Step Into Positivity

Remain solid as the winds and storms twirl around you. Jesus is the solid rock that cannot be moved. How do you feel when life is getting the best of you? What steps can you take to help strengthen you and push past your weaknesses?

_____

_____

_____

_____

_____

Prayer:

"God please fill my cup"

Scripture:

I can do all things through Christ which strengtheneth me. (Philippians 4:13)

JOY

Joy is a definite cure for the world's woes. Awaken each day knowing that you have been given a gift from our Heavenly Father and it's yours if you want it. Although everyone should have it, not all do. Joy is instilled within our souls so we can share it with others. Joy ignites like a wildfire when we show love and acceptance to our sisters and brothers. We witness this when we give a little baby a warm smile and the baby gives us a big smile back. That is unedited, uncensored joy!

As we grow in our spiritual walk with God, the joy of life grows with us. It shows up in a smile, a touch, in nature, and even in a dance. The joy of the Lord is contagious and can help you feel better and stronger. Joy is a Fruit of the Spirit. Do not let anyone steal your fruit- it belongs to you. Joy gives us clarity in our day to day lives. Without it we become bound with negativity. Pack joy with your prayers in your backpack, briefcase, purse, or lunch box and carry it through your day. Use joyous laughter as a weapon to get past trying moments. It's a guaranteed A!

Next Step:

The joy in my life comes to me like a colorful butterfly, with fluttering wings in the bright sun, pollinating beautiful blooming flowers. I love life and the people I share it with. They complete me and are a source of energy and joy. My joy radar also alerts me if this energy is being depleted. Life is a gift, and short, so I refuse to spend my time allowing the burdens of the world an opportunity to smother and rob me of my happiness. The world didn't give it and the world can't take it away.

123*456*78 - Step To The Rhythm Of Your Heart-

What does joy feel like to you? What could you do to rise to a new level of joy?

_____

_____

_____

Prayer:

"God let others see You when they see me."

Scripture:

Rejoice in the Lord always: *and* again I say, Rejoice. Let your moderation be known unto all men. The Lord *is* at hand. (Philippians 4:4-5)

PATIENCE

The common dominator of all true behavior is patience. This one is so hard for me and every day I get to practice it over, and over again! For years I struggled with immediate gratification, wanting everything to happen now! Pushing past myself seemed impossible at times; and every now and then, impatient thoughts still try and creep in. I'm learning to slow down, take a deep breath and wait. It's ok to wait, just as Jesus waits for us to cry out to Him so He can show us He really does exist to carry us through.

Next Steps:

Can you think of something that causes you to become anxious or lose control? What could you do to bring peace to your center core, to allow you a chance to breath and dance? First, begin by setting a foundation for your beliefs. Practice being patient for the desires of your heart. Do not allow the evil one to have power over what is good. Cast away all thoughts of negativity and disbelief before it creeps into your consciousness.

Rise each day feeling blessed and empowered with the amour of Jesus knowing that you have been given a special role to carry out the Faith another day. Wait on the Lord to deliver your gift of fulfillment through the Holy Spirit. There's no doubt that He will arrive right on time. Wait on those things that you desire and don't rush your life away with hurried actions; substitute your "now" with prayer to allow God to fill the gap.

123*456*78 - Step With Peace

Write your pressing "now" needs that you want God's help with. Tell Him how you will wait patiently for Him to reveal His true purpose in this area of your life.

_____

_____

_____

_____

_____

Prayer:

"God please help me learn to wait to gain clarity"

Scripture:

Wait on the Lord: be of good courage, and he shall strengthen thine heart: wait, I say, on the Lord. (Psalm 27:14)

FRIENDSHIP

The beauty of life and love blossoms when we come together in a way that makes God happy. He smiles upon us and captures our moments of true community. We were created to be one in love and family. Friendship is learning how to cultivate relationships that have true meaning and substance. The number one ingredient is to be genuine in every aspect; then you can watch your relationships and deep connections grow into lasting relationships. True friends can mend a broken heart, bring strength to those who are weak, comfort a grieving spirit, and ease the pain of a dying soul. Don't allow time or earthly battles to come between what is good and Godly - between you and a friend.

Next Steps:

We were all called to live in community (common-unity) so no one should have to go through this life alone. I've learned the value of this in my own relationships and have been blessed with great friendships. This is one of the greatest gifts I could ever receive from my Heavenly Father; having someone to share laughter and pain. My friends and I manage to stay true to the "why" of it all so that when the enemy tries to run interference in our relationships, we are quick to mend the cracks so we can get back to being there for each other.

123*456*78 - Step In Genuine Love

How can you step up to be a better friend in your relationships? What does true friendship look like to you?

_____

_____

Prayer:

"God please grow me to be a true friend"

Scripture:

Thine own friend, and thy father's friend, forsake not; neither go into thy brother's house in the day of thy calamity; *for* better *is* a neighbour that is near than a brother far off. (Proverbs 27:10)

DISCERNMENT

Learning how to dance involves learning the steps until it becomes second nature, until the movements become intuitive. Discernment is like learning how to dance with the Lord. Here's what I mean. You may be cautious of your surroundings or protect your heart from someone because something in you makes you hesitant. You're not sure why, but the "why" is revealed slowly, step by step.

Look for the presence, or absence, of God in all situations before you commit to anything or anyone. God should always be leading and guiding you, revealing His plans and purpose when He's ready. Discernment allows you to follow His lead. Once you acknowledge His presence wait for His whisper for your next move. He will never lead you into anything for spiteful causes.

Next Steps:

I was totally shocked when I learned that discernment is one of my spiritual gifts. I thought "wow", how is this possible? Over time I have come to realize my discernment is why it was always so hard for me not to be judgmental of the people and circumstances. It was because I could feel see and hear spiritually what others could (or would) not.

I have since learned to look through the eyes of Jesus to help me better understand people and have compassion for them. I'm learning to look for God's presence in everyone; and I'm learning that if He is nowhere in sight I proceed with caution. Listen carefully, open your eyes and mind, and remain vigilant. Don't allow your emotion to take you where your heart will not keep you.

Allow the Holy Spirit a chance to wash over your soul. If it doesn't move you the right way then take a step back and wait, allow God to reveal to you what you cannot see.

123*456*78 - Step With God

Do you allow others to impose their actions and attitudes before you can discern what is in front of you? What have been the consequences of your impulsiveness? Next time, where can you allow Jesus to enter into the picture?

_____

_____

_____

———————————————————

———————————————————

———————————————————

———————————————————

———————————————————

Prayer:

"Lord help me choose what is Godly"

Scripture:

My son, let not them depart from thine eyes: Keep sound wisdom and discretion: so shall they be life unto thy soul, and grace to thy neck. Then shalt thou walk in thy way safely, and thy foot shall not stumble. When thou liest down, thou shalt not be afraid: yea, thou shalt lie down, and thy sleep shall be sweet. (Proverbs 3:21-24)

LOVE

Like the vibrant colors of a butterfly, emotional love can cast a collage of feelings upon us. For the sake of this kind of carnal love we laugh or cry, celebrate or envy, we give and we take, and carry hearts that have open wounds that have not healed from past experiences. Although this love feels real, it is different from the spiritual truth of love which covers all past hurts and allows us to forgive. The greatest commandment "to love others as you love yourself" is also the greatest unconditional no strings tied gift you will ever receive. It's a gift you can give to anyone to promote healing, establish friendships, garner patience, hear the voice of discernment and more. When you have done your homework to really love yourself, flaws and all, you are then free to love others. Ask God to reveal his love to you and allow him a chance to show you true love then let him help you repair your brokenness so you can love in a healthy way. Put him first on your love list and all your relationships will blossom.

Next Steps:

It takes maturity to know the difference between emotional carnal love than the perfect love of God. I used to be deeply wounded when I was jilted by someone I loved - and it hurt badly for some time until I realized something. I could still be committed to loving them right where they were. while I stepped out of the way and let God take control of the situation. When I stepped out of the way, I moved into His loving assurance that He loves me and He cares for me, and He wanted me to love me too! Until you fall in love with yourself you will never understand what true love looks like from anyone else. Step out of the way and allow God an opportunity to restore what is broken.

123*456*78 - Step In The Footprints of Jesus

Do you have any love wounds or heartbreak? What can you do to heal yourself? What ways can you love yourself?

_____

_____

_____

_____

Prayer:

"God help me extend Grace"

Scripture:

Keep thy heart with all diligence; for out of it *are* the issues of life. (Proverbs 4:23)

PASSION

Express yourself boldly, savor the good things around you, and feed your spirit and soul with life! Awaken each day with the zest of a creature who travels through the jungle looking for his prey. One must stay focused and in control to conquer, show poise as others look on, and take charge of your emotions. Wrap your heart around your desires and go for it.

Let your actions match your desire to accept what rocks your heart. Pour all of your love into what you desire knowing that when you do you will bring a smile upon the face of Jesus. He loves to see us give our all to something good.

Next Steps:

Dance came naturally to me at an early age. As I grew older, my love of dance was planted in my heart with a passion that shaped my world and connected me with the beauty of each step. This is the same beauty I feel when called to serve others - another passion of mine.

Each day I awaken with the thoughts of the beauty in serving others in need, whether its collecting shoes from friends and delivering them to our Church Care Center, serving at Church, or helping with community fundraisers. I feel so complete when I'm helping others. This is how I know that serving is my passion. I step boldly into servanthood.

123*456*78 - Step with Desire

What greater cause than yourself do you feel called to step up to? What are your reasons that hold you back? What steps will you take to connect you to your passion?

_____

_____

_____

_____

_____

_____

_____

_____

Prayer:

"God please do not let my greed overpower my desires"

Scripture:

With good will doing service, as to the Lord, and not to men: Knowing that whatsoever good thing any man doeth, the same shall he receive of the Lord, whether *he be* bond or free. (Ephesians 6:7,8)

CELEBRATE AND DANCE

Celebrate your life. It's easy! Just look up to the sky and pick out your dancing cloud. Follow its form and see how it takes shape and glides into the sunlight to form bright beaming rays upon the onlookers in life. Now, place your feet, one before the other, spread your arms like wings and listen to the beat in your heart. Start your celebration dance!!

Next Steps:

Match the beat of your soul to the beat of your heart then come into a perfect harmony with who you really are. Remember to live each day by the lyrics of your life, shaping your thoughts and actions along the way. Tap into your spirit and dance through life in a way that says, "I'm free"! Move through each day with God controlling your steps, gently guiding you into greatness. Live your best day each day.

123*456*78 - Step In The Name Of Jesus

When was the last time you celebrated yourself? Write down all your accomplishments, big and small. At the end of the week, read them to yourself and do a victory dance and repeat!

_____

_____

Prayer:

"God please lead me in my Steps"

Scripture:

There is a time for everything, and a season for every activity under heaven: 2 a time to be born and a time to die, a time to plant and a time to uproot, 3 a time to kill and a time to heal, a time to tear down and a time to build, 4 a time to weep and a time to laugh, a time to mourn and a time to dance. (Ecclesiastes-3:1-4)

And this day shall be unto you for a memorial; and ye shall keep it a feast to the Lord throughout your generations; ye shall keep it a feast by an ordinance for ever. (Exodus 12:14)

ABOUT THE AUTHOR

If you can identify with the spirit of a butterfly, then you already know Debbie Welch for she is on the move and making things happen! Like a butterfly, she pollinates everything she lands upon. She is bright and spirited, filled with the joy and love of life. Debbie's upbeat attitude and energetic personality keep her in tune to the crazy beats of her busy world. Debbie is a mother of three, grandmother of ten, and great-grandmother of five and has a heart for God, family and friends.

Originally from a small Alabama town, Debbie moved to the Chicago where she earned a master's degree in Corrections and Criminal Justice from Chicago State University. In addition, she joined with the Chicago Urban League to mentor inner city youth and spent time working as a counselor with troubled youths. A true people person, Debbie started Red Carpet Shoe Boutique, and created a meeting place where women gathered to shop in a fun filled environment, while organizing fundraising dance events for a local women's shelter. This is where she began hosting an advanced weekly dance group called "The Next Level Stepper's".

Debbie carries a strong passion in her heart for dance, feeling as if Jesus is guiding her every step. She is a competitive dancer and former member of the "Rock City Unique Stepper's" dance group (Rockford, IL) and the "Northwest Stepper's" group of Hoffman Estates IL. When Debbie isn't dancing or serving at her Willow Creek Church, she loves cooking, reading and writing.

"Stepping Into Faith" is Debbie's first book and is rooted in her passion for dance and helping others. Currently Debbie is retired from the federal government and is an independent contractor in the financial services industry. When asked for a few words to share with her readers, she replies:

"Remember to Dance"

Made in the USA
Columbia, SC
23 November 2020